God of Evil King Manasseh

W. D. Crowder

ISBN: 9781793156242

DEDICATION

This book is lovingly dedicated to my two beloved children Irina (13) and
Alex (7). You both give me the extra incentive, motivation, and reason to
get up early every morning to make time to write these beautiful stories of
God's everlasting faithfulness to His heroes that I so love to write about.
God will never abandon you my dear sweet children Alex and Irina, not in
your whole lives here on earth or in the everlasting one to come!

CONTENTS

ACKNOWLEDGMENTS

I want to thank all of my faithful tens of thousands of readers of the Heroes of the Faith Daily Devotional Series written and published 5 days per week on average for the Facebook Christian Forums. Your interaction, encouragement, and prayers helped motivate me to finally get on to this book that has been in the works for years now, ever since I wrote the *Three Miraculous Prayers of King Hezekiah* back in 2013. God bless and keep you all!

1 INTRODUCTION

An unlikely Biblical hero is the subject of this new book you hold in your hands. If you are looking for a role model of a man you can literally relate to, a man who prayed for the strength to make enormous Godly changes in his own failed life, then look no further than the man who God once called most wicked of all the kings of Judah. Manasseh practiced sorcery and divination, consulted with mediums and necromancers, gleefully shed innocent blood, sacrificed his own children in fire to the detestable god Molech, and has rightfully so gone down in infamy as the man who ordered Isaiah the prophet--- friend and counselor of his own great Godly father King Hezekiah--- to be killed. Manasseh didn't just execute the Prophet Isaiah either, he had him sawed in two with a wooden saw.

The day of reckoning finally came for King Manasseh when God stirred the hated evil Assyrian empire against him. They put a hook through Manasseh's nose, chained him, and dragged him behind a chariot thousands of kilometers to captivity in Babylon, where they unceremoniously threw what remained of the man into the terrifying dark dungeons that no one ever emerged from alive.

This was a man that everyone had written off completely by this point. No one would have ever guessed that he would completely turn from his entrenched evil past and wicked ways while at this rock bottom, darkest of places. Yet the story is most interesting and relevant to us today exactly because Manasseh did something that no one at all expected--- in this darkest place, he prayed desperately to his God and the God of his mighty prayer warrior father Hezekiah for mercy, forgiveness, and deliverance. God met him more than halfway, so impressed by his prayer that concentrated around one incredible line: "Although I am not worthy, You will save me according to Your great mercy."

It was then that Manasseh found the miraculous strength to make amazing Godly changes in his life! The Assyrians incredibly not only released him from the dark dungeons but also sent him home to rule his Kingdom of Judah once again. Manasseh who had been the most wicked king of all then spent the remainder of his reign undoing the evils of his youth.

He became a role model of repentance who made a 180 degree change for the great God of the universe and of all mankind! As you read through the pages of this book about the true story of a ruined man who needed the goodness and mercy of God in his life desperately, remember this eternal truth: God alone is good, and He is good all the time, no matter how hopeless, lost, and dark things may appear in your own life today!

2 AN UNEXPECTED TIME TRAVELING ODYSSEY

The time traveling Odyssey is a marvel of modern day technology, an amazing discovery that allows you to personally experience the wonders of the glorious past with all of its triumphs and tragedies. As you curiously climb in and sit down at the control panel, you hear more than see the machine suddenly hum to life. Before you can react, the door closes and locks, a seatbelt connects around your waist, and the main console screen starts flashing urgently one single word in red. It reads, "MANASSEH" in screaming bold letters.

You scratch your head, wondering who or what is a Manasseh? Admitting honestly to yourself that history has never been your strongest study, you settle back for the ride that appears to no longer be optional. Some minutes later you awaken in surprise and discover to your horror that the Odyssey has abandoned you, lying on a hill overlooking a whitewashed walled city. There is nothing left for you to do but to head into the fortified town.

The next thing you notice is that your clothes have changed

drastically. You do not remember slipping into an ancient world looking robe and sandals, but there is now nothing to do but to play along with the unfolding scenario surrounding you. The burning question in your mind is: Where are you? As you enter the massive city gates of the bustling town, you realize the more appropriate query might instead be: When are you?

Closing your eyes a moment, the last thing that you remember was the flashing single red word MANASSEH on the console main screen. It is the only clue that you have in your possession, so you walk over to a market stall and ask the fruit seller of dates, olives, and pomegranates, "Manasseh?"

The large and muscled man studies you hard for a long, slow moment, giving your colorful robes and sandals a once over before losing interest and growing bored. He then waves his arm up the hill to what looks like a palace sitting near some sort of enormous temple structure. It may still be early in the morning judging by the position of the rising sun, but the streets are already flooding with throngs of people wearing robes and sandals not unlike your own. Waving your thanks to the man, you head up the street, taking in the sites and smells of this clearly ancient world city as you gradually approach the temple and palace looming above over all.

Another inquiry along the way confirms your destination is the palace near the temple. Yet the day is early, and this Manasseh might not be awake and receiving visitors yet, so you decide to wander into the temple first. A little sightseeing might provide some clues on where you actually are. Realizing that the Odyssey has simply left you here, you nervously push aside the nagging thought that this is where you now live.

The temple is enormous, easily the largest building inside this walled city. Priests are busy with some sort of morning ritual. Everywhere you look, you see conflicting signs. There are a number of different alters and grotesque statue figures set up in the courtyard. Animals are being led to what looks like it will be a literal slaughter as the priests prepare their morning animal sacrifices to a number of differing deities. Feeling your stomach unsettling, you decide quickly that maybe this is enough of temple sightseeing for one morning.

Moments later, you find yourself in front of the palace gates. Before you have a chance to seek out the gate guards, you suddenly hear a long, low horn blast. Suddenly the palace gates are violently thrown open and a procession emerges from within. So much for thinking this Manasseh might still be sleeping! Clearly that persistent horn and the ensuing dramatic, loud music would waken even the dead.

Men mounted on horseback emerge at the head of a processional column. They are carrying banners depicting a five pointed blue star on a white background. Remembering your Sunday school lessons, you gasp in a sudden flood of recognition. That is the star of King David of Israel! This must be Jerusalem the ancient capital and city of David. The nagging question is: Who is this Manasseh?

You do not have to wonder for long. Moments later you see a man seated on a throne riding atop a platform type of bearer vehicle. Arrayed in purple robes and with a golden crown gracing his head, you realize that this must be him. You study this obviously King Manasseh, determined to understand a first impression about the man you have been sent back in time to find.

If appearances reveal anything about a person's inner heart and soul, then you do not much like what you see. The man's face is twisted in a dark scowl as he surveys his capital on a clear blue morning. His eyes dart furtively from side to side, all too clearly resembling a hunter seeking out his next victim.

It is his eyes that captivate you most though. They are hard and evil. As the procession passes directly by where you stand, you see for the first time two men who look like nothing so much as sorcerers or wizards flanking this Manasseh's royal throne to the rear. If they are his advisers, then you had best tread with caution. They look only slightly more evil than the occupant of the throne himself.

Swallowing nervously, you realize that you had better think through a meeting with this man whose Hebrew language you will not even understand. It might be smarter to keep a low profile and study him and his court for a few days first. Surely they have a weekly audience where petitioners can come into the palace and speak with the king.

Maybe you had better try to blend in as one of the innocent members of this crowd and come back to the palace on a day when he holds his royal court. As you ponder this idea, you watch the man's procession heading into the temple courtyard and you begin to understand. He is going to participate in those unpleasant-looking animal blood sacrifices. At least they are not live human sacrifices, you muse thoughtfully. It can always get worse.

Shaking your head in confusion, you follow along with a gathering crowd into the temple courtyard once more, but at a safe distance this time. As you see the ruler clearly prostrating himself before a particularly grotesque looking idol wreathed in flames, in bewilderment you wonder again (and not for the last time), just who exactly is this King Manasseh of Jerusalem, and what darkness troubles him so to make him look like such a despicable villain?

Taking in the troubling blood-soaked animal sacrifices scene unfolding all around you again, you have a sinking feeling that you will soon find out more than you want to know, and that you will not like the answer one bit.

3 WHO IS THIS EVIL KING MANASSEH?

When you awaken next, it is unclear whether you have slept one night or many of them. As you fight down malevolent thoughts against the faithless time traveling Odyssey that abandoned you here in Manasseh's strange, magical Kingdom of Judah, you wonder how long you will be trapped here.

It makes no sense just hiding and idling away the days though, so you spend the time as if you are here on a mission. Maybe that is what the Odyssey intended for you after all. It might be that this King Manasseh needs help with something.

On the second day here, you discovered by accident that somehow you understand and speak ancient Hebrew. It must have been some cruel joke from the Odyssey when it stranded you here. You stood close enough behind Manasseh in the temple to overhear him saying something to one of the priests and understood it.

The more you carefully shadow him, the less he seems a happy and well-balanced king of this little Kingdom of David. You remember enough about Judah from Sunday School to figure something is not right. All is not well in this land, starting from the king and trickling all the way down to his subjects.

Every time you follow him into the temple, you can not shake that nervous and uncomfortable feeling that something is really wrong here. This is the fabled Temple of King Solomon, the splendid house of God itself. Why entering it behind King Manasseh gives your stomach a queasy sick feeling is beyond your understanding at first.

Yet after a few such mornings of coming over to see the daily rituals and animal sacrifices you think you start to understand the reason why it makes you feel so uncomfortable. Something really is wrong here. You remember from your weekly Sunday School lessons that the people of Judah and Jerusalem worshiped the one true God Jehovah.

Clearly that is not what is going on here anymore under this King Manasseh. The man is young and may just be sowing his proverbial "royal wild oats," but you have already figured out from a half dozen mornings behind him in the temple that he and the people are not just worshipping one God any longer, not at all.

You have counted sacrifices to a half dozen different grotesque looking deities so far. It only takes a single look into the faces of these idols to realize that these are evil gods. Animal sacrifice is one thing, but you are becoming increasingly nervous that something more foul is imminent. For one thing, Manasseh has some kind of running argument going on with one of the priests who attends the statue wreathed in flames.

There is another deity erected to the worship of the stars. This seems to be a favorite of King Manasseh's. What you can not figure is who is worshipping Jehovah now? Wasn't this the reason that King Solomon, Manasseh's ancestor by a few hundred years only, built this temple in the first place? The only remnant of this original worship you still see here are the animal sacrifices, but clearly they are not offering them to Jehovah any longer.

Instead, they seem to be divided between serving this detestable god Molech of the fire, an astral Ashteroth pole, Marduk, Baal, and the starry host of the heavens. Watching the rituals, it looks increasingly barbaric to your modern day Judeo-Christian sensibilities. As you leave the temple again this morning wrapped in thought, you still can not figure out what has gone wrong in this ancient God-fearing kingdom of Southern Israel.

You have attended King Manasseh's weekly court a few times as well now. It has become increasingly clear that more is wrong in this kingdom than simply the idol worship. You were always taught in history class that kings existed to uphold justice and the law as well as to protect their people.

Manasseh does not seem to be interested in impartial justice. His two wizardly looking advisers turn out to be soothsayers and stargazers for one thing. Any idea of following the laws of Moses that God set out for the Kingdom of Judah to obey seem to have been abandoned completely under this young king.

This particular morning, you watch in shock and horror as Manasseh perverts justice most egregiously. This time, he has sentenced a few of Jehovah God's priests to death for some trivial sounding offence that appears to be clearly more imagined than real. What is more upsetting is that they will not simply be executed; they are to be offered as human sacrifices to that detestable fiery god Molech at the ritual sacrifices next week. You have decided that this can not be allowed. The wheels are turning rapidly in your head as you concoct a plan to rescue the priests and set them free.

Your plan is made easier by the fact that you seem to have some strange supernatural powers yourself in this timeless country. For one thing, the only people who are able to see you are the ones you actually want to see you. To everyone else here in Jerusalem you appear to be invisible.

If you do not speak to them, they simply see through you. Ignoring the potential ramifications of this, you choose to focus on the positive aspects of it as you wander through the dungeon beneath the king's Jerusalem palace late that night. Getting in and out yourself is easy. Taking care of the guards would be a problem if they could see you, but to your relief, they can not either. A few sharp blows to their heads takes care of Manasseh's prison guards.

The priests are relieved to see you and are on their hands and knees thanking Jehovah God for sparing them from human sacrifice to the detestable god Molech. It turns out that they were sentenced to death before him for speaking out against the deity. King Manasseh had given them a last chance to recant and fall down in abject worship of Molech, but they have steadfastly refused to offer animal or human blood sacrifices to the evil god of the Canaanites.

You can hardly blame them. The fiery idol seems to be some kind of an intensively hot oven that has a the form of a god constructed over and around it. Listening to the screams and watching the thrashings of the animals thrown onto it was bad enough. You can not imagine the scene being repeated with living people thrown on there. As you and the priests of the One True God quietly and stealthily leave the dungeon, you breathe a sigh of relief. Rescuing them was partly the result of your motive to not have to see innocent human beings burned to death while still alive on that hated monstrous false god's form.

The priests are overjoyed, and they take you to stay in some sort of a safe house with them in the old city. This humble hide out beats the simple room you have been sheltering in since you arrived in Jerusalem however many days ago it was. It is then that you realize that you have completely lost count of the days you spend here in Judah. For one thing, you are never certain that you sleep only a single night away when you lie down each evening after dark.

As they pour out their sordid tale, the priests begin to open your eyes about the true evil of King Manasseh. Apparently he is the greatest paradox the ancient world has ever known in human form. The man became king at only 12 years old.

He took the throne from his revered and beloved mighty prayer warrior of a hero father King Hezekiah. From what the priests tell you with tears in their eyes, Hezekiah was as good and valiant as his wayward son Manasseh is evil and depraved.

Hezekiah had cried out to God all of his adult life for help and miracles. More amazingly still, you listen to incredible tales of the supernatural ways his God answered him his entire life. These started when King Hezekiah was holding a great Passover Feast.

At the week plus long festival celebrated by not just the people of the Kingdom of Judah and all Jerusalem but also the remnants of the people left in the now defunct Northern Kingdom of Israel, many of the Jewish people came to partake of the feast before God without having completed the crucial purification rights and ceremonies that God had prescribed in the laws of Moses. The penalty for this was instant death. You watch the priests' eyes shining as they recount how King Hezekiah saw many thousands of attendees sickening and dying before his very eyes that first day of the feast.

Rather than shrink in terror, he rose up and cried aloud to God to have mercy on all those people who had personally prepared their hearts to come worship and seek Him. Jehovah God heard King Hezekiah's prayer, and the people were healed, forgiven, and spared!

The priests spend the rest of the night telling you of the other two incredible miracles God did for His friend and servant King Hezekiah. Once, an enormous enemy army of nearly 200,000 angry enemy soldiers came thousands of miles from the Assyrian Empire. They had death, destruction, and conquest on their minds. No one could stop them.

Their evil King Sennacharib sent a death threat letter to Hezekiah, who famously took the parchment into the temple of God and spread it out before the Lord. Hezekiah reminded God that the wicked king was far more powerful than his own army, and that this Sennacharib had insulted not only the Kingdom of Judah and people of Jerusalem with his written and verbal affronts, but the living almighty God of the universe. King Hezekiah appealed to God to overthrow the enemy and save him and his people.

God responded that night with an Angel of the Lord passing over the Assyrian army with the vengeance of God. When Sennacharib woke up the next morning, 185,000 Assyrian soldiers did not arise. The evil Assyrian ruler who had boasted that he would overthrow Jehovah God found himself climbing back into his own chariot and driving like mad all the way back home to his capital Nineveh as fast as humanly possible. Within a month of his disgraced return, his own two sons had conspired against and murdered him while he worshiped the false Assyrian god Marduk in that temple in Nineveh.

In the last fifteen years of King Hezekiah Manasseh's father's life and reign, the great Godly king had become sick with a wasting illness, the priests tell you as the night begins to wane. Hezekiah had received a visit from his faithful friend and counselor Isaiah the Prophet of God. Isaiah had come to comfort his old friend and beloved king in his illness and distress. Unfortunately, God gave Isaiah the word to tell King Hezekiah to put his house in order, for he was going to die and not recover. Hezekiah ordered everyone to leave the room, and Isaiah sadly started to depart from the palace complex for his own home.

Meanwhile, King Hezekiah faced the wall and cried aloud to his God, "I have walked faithfully and loyally before you my whole life." The great man of God began to weep. In moments, Isaiah who was just in the outer courtyard of the palace had a message from God to turn around and return to His servant Hezekiah with a new and better word of encouragement.

Isaiah burst back into the room in joy to tell the great king that God was going to heal him completely, and that on the third day he would be back in the temple of God worshipping him again. God would give him another 15 years added on to his life. The priests have a fire burning in their eyes as they recount the miraculous sign God gave King Hezekiah that all of this would come to pass. Jehovah offered to move time forward or backward for the king. Hezekiah chose to have time move back 12 hours.

The rescued priests sadly sigh as they conclude the true story. Shaking their heads, they spread their arms before you and ask you how such a mighty valiant man of God could sire such an evil son in Manasseh. Since he assumed the throne at 12 years old, he has done nothing but undo all the good of his father's kingdom in exchange for as much imported evil as he could manage.

He has profaned the sacred temple of God with idols and foreign deities. Priests who were consecrated to only the worship of Jehovah God have been forced into the service of these detestable gods like Molech and Ashteroth. If they refuse the new work, Manasseh finds a reason to accuse them of crimes or even high treason against the crown.

Shuddering, the priests tell you how they were not the first ones to have their blood shed on the oven-idol of Molech. It has become an all too common occurrence in fact. The priests fear for their brothers' safety, as an enraged Manasseh may seize them instead to sacrifice on the idol of his violent god in their places.

You sigh and shake your head. You can not count on another daring midnight rescue through the dungeons. Manasseh will double the guards in the future when he has prisoners that he can not afford to let escape.

As the sun is beginning to dawn, the priests prepare a place for you to sleep near them. They shake their heads and tell you that Manasseh is planning a more spectacular and epic human sacrifice to Molech in two weeks' time. They worry who the victim will be, fearing that it will be an innocent member of his own family, someone close to him. That would be a terrible, true sacrifice.

As you lie there listening to the early morning sounds of the city of Jerusalem awakening, you fall into a troubled sleep in which the soldiers of King Manasseh chase you around the capital Jerusalem threatening to sacrifice you on the alter of the evil god Molech when they finally catch you.

4 THE ULTIMATE HUMAN BLOOD SACRIFICE TO MOLECH

With each passing day, you watch transfixed in morbid fascination and horror as things only seem to go from bad to worse in what you now call King Manasseh's reign of terror. No one in the capital city Jerusalem seems to be having a good time but him. Blood is starting to run down the proverbial city streets as this sick man literally fills Jerusalem with bloodshed from one end to another. And yet no one seems capable of stopping him or even challenging his murderous policies. If Manasseh's father King Hezekiah could see him now, he would be rolling over in his grave, you say as you shake your head in utter disgust.

You only thought things were bad in the kingdom before this morning though. It was today that you witnessed an all-time low as the wicked King Manasseh embarked on a terrible spectacle to his fire wreathed god Molech he had set up in the courtyard of the temple of the Living God. The king had been using his political enemies and prisoners as fodder for the insatiable blood lust appetite of the monstrous idol and his equally bloodthirsty priests. Today he ran out of sacrificial victims, so he turned to one that you had never expected.

King Manasseh entered the temple this morning like most mornings, with the strange difference that he had his firstborn son with him today. You knew something was wrong immediately when you saw the young child prince enter the temple with his hands bound behind his back and a look of abject terror on his face. A sickening feeling rising in the pit of your stomach told you what was about to happen, but you had to witness it personally to actually believe the man was capable of this act of barbaric atrocity.

Approaching the alter of Molech with his son in tow, the king was busy with some words of enraptured worship and devotion one moment. The next thing anyone watching knew, he had forcefully seized his now struggling eldest son by the shoulders and was shoving him roughly towards the grotesque murdering deity. It took the intervention of a few of Manasseh's brawny soldiers, but no one in the crowd or the entourage at all moved to stop the monster of a king as he had his own son hauled up on the fiery alter and then stood approving close by to personally watch the horrible struggle and hear his son's screams as he burned to death before the gathered assemblage this morning.

To watch the wicked king's behavior and reaction, it was just another day at the office. The muted expressions on the assemblage's faces did not betray their feelings. Undoubtedly they were only happy he had not managed to somehow find an excuse to seize and sacrifice their own children to this monstrosity of an idol, for today at least. How much longer could this evil be tolerated and permitted to continue under heaven, you wonder as your head starts spinning?

Running from the Temple of Jehovah God who would never condone such a terrible atrocity, much less human sacrifice at all, you forcefully empty the contents of your stomach just outside the temple entrance. In moments you have broken into a run for the place where you hide out with Jehovah's out of favor priests. You do not want to see anymore spectacle this morning, only to get far away from the monster of a man who just willingly murdered his own firstborn son, making a mockery of the temple, city, and kingdom of the One True God of all mankind.

How much longer can it go on, and when will someone from somewhere, anywhere at all, finally put an end to this seemingly never ending climax of atrocities committed by this enemy of human decency King Manasseh, you wonder aloud. As you relate the sordid morning tale to the priests with the bile rising in your stomach again, you hear a commotion coming outside of the safe house. In the streets, you and your friend priests witness the powerful arrival of a man who has grim determination plainly written on his features.

You wonder who this man boldly marching towards the palace complex could be? Whoever he is, it takes a tremendous amount of courage for anyone to willingly go see the wicked King Manasseh on these sacrifice mornings, in particular on the grim day where he murdered his oldest son just to satisfy the blood lust of a god that no one in their right mind could ever venerate, much less openly tolerate. The priests seem excited by the arrival of the grimly determined man moving purposefully now towards the palace of the king. When you arch an eyebrow, they answer you who this stranger is.

The legendary Prophet Isaiah-- friend, counselor, and spiritual mentor to the father of Manasseh, the late King Hezekiah-- has come at long last. Isaiah will finally put a stop to the senseless and wanton blood letting before Molech, the priests assure you. He is the only one in the entire kingdom with the courage and presence to stand up before the king and talk him back off of the proverbial ledge.

You become so curious that you have to go see this impending showdown and contest of wills for yourself. The priests decline to put themselves in harm's way, sure the king would recognize them if he caught a glimpse of their faces again in an audience that includes the Prophet Isaiah. So it is that you set out alone for the palace of the kings of Judah, anxious to hear what the Prophet Isaiah will say to this chief of sinners regarding his idol worship.

Apparently you are not alone in your morbid curiosity and fascination. Half the city of Jerusalem must be thronging the city streets all at once right now. It is just as well the Jehovah God priests did not come with you, for you would surely have been hopelessly separated by the surging crowd pressing in from every direction. On your own, you finally just give in and allow the mob to carry you along in the press of humanity, inexorably closer to the impending showdown at the Jerusalem palace of King David.

In the great audience of hall of the kings of Judah, Manasseh sits determinedly on his throne. To feel the tension in the room, you decide this must be the first meeting between the lord of the land and the spiritual advisor and messenger from God to this sinful, wayward son of a righteous father Hezekiah. King Manasseh does not look happy to see him one bit. As Isaiah steps forward, given the debatable honor of being first to address the sovereign, you can hear the tangible silence and cut the tension in the room with a knife.

Isaiah begins to speak, holding his arms aloft to declaim his warning message to the unworthy son of the great King Hezekiah. He tells the young monarch that his evils have become so great with that morning's sacrifice to Molech that God can no longer stand the stench of Manasseh in His holy city of Jerusalem and temple. God in His unfailing mercy has opted to provide Manasseh with a dire warning and a second chance to repent and turn from his vile ways.

Isaiah shouts in a loud, clear, unbroken voice that clearly carries across the packed full audience chamber as he warns the evil king. Manasseh must stop all of the human sacrifices to the despicable god Molech, remove all idols from the courtyard of God's Temple, and stop the incessant perversion of justice that has become a hallmark of the first 15 years of Manasseh's bloodthirsty reign of terror. If he does not cease the evil practices immediately, Manasseh will be handed over by a wrathful and righteous God to his enemies the dreaded Assyrians. Isaiah promises grimly that they will chain the young king and take him away to life long torment in the dark of the Assyrians' imperial dungeons from which no one has ever before escaped or been released.

A stunned silence descends on the hushed crowd as they take

in the full effect of the Prophet Isaiah's declamation. The righteous old man has just issued a fearless ultimatum and warning to the man who did not hesitate to murder his own son that very morning in a manner most horrible and cruel. Studying Manasseh's hands, you can see them turning white as he grips the arm rests of the throne with knuckles changing color in his fury. It does not look like it will go well for the brave, lonely figure of Isaiah the prophet this morning.

Sure enough, Manasseh explodes in pent up rage. He orders Isaiah seized and imprisoned himself. The guards hesitate a moment as they watch the righteous prophet fearlessly standing his ground, arms still outstretched in final ominous warning.

Manasseh leaps to his feet and runs toward Isaiah himself. With a wicked smile on his face, he rubs gleeful hands together and decries that Isaiah shall be the victim in tomorrow morning's human sacrifice to the fire god. Manasseh reminds Isaiah as they chain him and take him away to the dungeon that he has less than 24 hours to make his peace with God and get ready to go meet his maker personally. No one escapes the terror and judgment of Molech the god of fire, Manasseh shrieks in barely contained rage.

Unsurprisingly, the crowd looks stunned. By ones and twos, and then in increasing numbers, the people of Jerusalem and Judah quickly melt away from the scene of judgment and doom. No one there had expected to hear the death sentence pronounced on the revered and legendary prophet that morning. Isaiah in many ways had represented the best and last hope for the city and kingdom of God. Yet his dire warnings have had their intended impact on the people who are quickly leaving lest Manasseh's displeasure fall on anyone else gathered there.

No doubt they are all thinking on the warning of Isaiah. If the Assyrians return, the same Assyrians who God defeated and destroyed for the righteous King Hezekiah, it is not likely to bode well for the people of the city of Jerusalem, much less the rest of the Kingdom of Judah. You stealthily creep back to the hideaway safe house on the outskirts of the old city to share the terrible news with the priests, who will no doubt be devastated.

Isaiah had been their personal hero since most of them were mere boys aspiring to follow in his footsteps and serve the God of their fathers. Now you have to bear the terrible tidings back to them of his impending doom with the dawn tomorrow. You pass a most uneasy night's sleep as all of the visions of an Assyrian invasion race through your head in retaliation for the latest and greatest evil that wicked King Manasseh has set in motion concerning God's righteous spokesman of the age for the kingdom. Will no one intervene to save not just a good man, but indeed God's righteous man, you wonder aloud to yourself?

5 THE COLD BLOODED MURDER OF ISAIAH THE PROPHET

You stir uneasily the next morning as the roosters awaken you with their incessant crowing. They at least are not dismayed to face the dawning of the day that will witness the untimely demise of the Prophet Isaiah. Where is the God of King Hezekiah now?

Why will He not intervene to save what is apparently His only righteous man in all of the Kingdom of Judah still possessing the courage and resolve to stand up to this monster of a young monarch? These are questions that consume your soul as you eat some bread and prepare to go watch the latest human sacrifice blasphemy to the horrible idol Molech in the temple courtyard of God.

When you arrive, you notice at once that the procedures for the morning are different than what you have witnessed every other human sacrifice morning. For one thing, there is no smoke and fire wreaths coiling hatefully around the grotesque idol Molech. You try to push closer for a better look, but the crowds are absolutely enormous today. Whatever people individually think of the Prophet Isaiah, he commands enough respect to bring out everyone who does not have somewhere else that they have to be this morning.

The horrible ordeal commences with the arrival of wicked King Mansseh. He looks both well-rested and most pleased to witness the destruction of his arch-enemy. As Isaiah comes in under a heavy guard, hands bound behind his back and defiance still glowering in every feature, Manasseh rubs his hands together in glee. Yet the fires on Molech are not lit. How will they sacrifice anyone like that?

The king is giving a long-rehearsed speech now. He says that in an extra special torment for this morning's rebellious victim, Molech will not be lit and fired until after Isaiah is tied atop the idol's outstretched arms. They lay the bound prophet in the horrible last embrace of the bloodthirsty god of fire and back away. Long, slow minutes pass and still nothing has happened. Staring hard at the terrible idol, it dawns on you that the fires are still not lit.

There is a brief commotion as the priests approach Manasseh, torches still burning in their hands. Apparently the fire god is not up to the challenge this particular morning. They can not get him lit and heating.

Manasseh's frustration and dangerously mounting fury is obvious as he seizes a pair of torches and strides boldly down to the back of the idol himself. You can not clearly see his actions, but he appears to be personally attempting to stoke the fires of Molech himself. By the expression of dismay and súrprise on his face, he seems to be having no more success than the frightened priests this morning.

Try as they might, none of them can get Molech to light in order to burn Isaiah the Prophet to death. The crowd stands by looking on in stunned silence. Moments later you start to hear whispers passing through the crowds. It is a miracle! Jehovah God will not allow Molech to consume His personal spokesman the prophet today!

Wicked King Manasseh stands aghast, briefly at a loss for words and for what to do about the situation he seems to be quickly losing control of as he stands there dumb stricken. Manasseh may be many things, but a fool he is not. He soon confers urgently with the priests about their next plan of action. You can see him at first frustrated, then his features warming and twisting into an evil smile as a new thought has occurred to the young monarch.

Hands raised to quiet the murmuring crowd, he explains that they have decided on a special spectacle worthy of the execution of the Prophet Isaiah so that everyone in the kingdom will know who is king and who is not. Manasseh has abandoned lighting up Molech for that morning, and no doubt he has learned a lesson regarding waiting to stoke up the fires until the time has actually arrived for the daily human sacrifice. Undeterred, he holds up a wooden instrument of some kind in the air, waving it wildly around as the priests start some kind of onerous chanting.

You are not familiar with this alternate ritual which they are starting to perform, but by the looks of the jagged teeth on this wooden implement the king is pumping in the air over his head, you figure the final end for Isaiah will be anything but pleasant. Jehovah God has already intervened to save him by quieting the grotesque idol this morning. Will He stop Manasseh and his priests from physically hacking the man of God to pieces now too?

As you ponder this grim question, Manasseh turns and hands the what is apparently a wooden bone saw of some kind to the chief priest of Molech. The king takes a step closer to flash an evil smile to Isaiah before standing a step back to enjoy the death of his most bitter enemy. Manasseh raises his voice in a triumphant cry as they get to work on the poor prophet, who so far is managing not to scream as they begin literally sawing him in half.

This is what happens to those who set themselves higher than or gainsay the king, Manasseh has decried. It takes only a moment for you to realize what is happening as a piercing cry rips from the old prophet's throat. Clearly the saw is working better than the fire god lighting did. Blood is fountaining in all directions, covering the priests of Molech from their arms to their heads.

You look away, unable to watch the horror unfolding before you as they literally hack the aged prophet to death. Long before the murder climaxes, you have pushed your way forcibly back out of the crowd and left the temple. If you hear Isaiah's final death rattle, you fear you may never get the horrifying sound and ceremony out of your mind again. Something like this barbarity could haunt a person's dreams for the rest of their lives.

As you walk slowly and heavily back to the hidden safe house of the priests of Jehovah, you shake your head in dismay and wonder. God did not save the innocent son of Manasseh from the arms of Molech the terrible yesterday. He would not let a false god murder his last great prophet today, but He did not stop Manasseh's foul priests from sawing him apart this morning.

Now there is no one left alive who would dare oppose the regime of this increasingly bloodthirsty tyrant of Jerusalem. The penalty for doing so is an excruciatingly painful end as part of a horrible daily ritual spectacle in front of the eyes of the people in God's own holy temple.

Only a fool would dare to oppose such an evil and powerful man, you think as you shake your head. You have seen enough of this God forsaken kingdom of Judah as you wander back to the safe house. If only the time traveling Odyssey had not abandoned you in this tiny kingdom, you would quickly put it all behind you.

But as you ponder why you are here and what you are meant to do in this land, the thought occurs to you that something significant is about to transpire here. Isaiah's warnings of curses he had declaimed on King Manasseh but a day before surely will not fall on deaf ears of the almighty God of Israel.

You decide to talk this over with the priests of Jehovah, all of who are up and about when you return from the ritual. They gaze at you with hope and longing as you return, desperate to hear that God has performed a miracle to save the chief of their kind in Judah. After you sadly shake your head no, you begin to pour out the grisly tail of the end of the mighty Prophet Isaiah.

Tears are streaming down the faces of these men who generally loved him like a father figure. The death of Isaiah represents the end of a once-glorious era for Judah. The man had sought out a righteous servant of God for king of God's little kingdom, and he found him at last in King Hezekiah.

But the king is long dead now these past 15 years; long live the king. Unfortunately that new king is more monster than man now. As you talk over the tragic events of the morning with the weeping priests, you wonder aloud again how such a bloodthirsty murderer could ever have been the direct scion of a mighty prayer warrior like good King Hezekiah? Could the venerable king been such a poor father figure as to ignore Manasseh like a youth until he turned his heart against both his legendary father and His own God?

No one has a ready answer. It is a day for mourning and sorrow, and even the heavens reflect this now. What started as a bright and promising day has changed into a sad, slow rain that would wash away all the blood letting and evil of the monster king. As you ponder all of this, you realize that no amount of rain can wash away the stain of the innocently shed blood of the great Prophet Isaiah though. Nothing can atone for this outrage before the God of Heaven that you have personally witnessed today.

The priests refuse to lose all hope, despite the death of their hero and ultimate head of their order. Personally you are not so sure. What gives you hope is discussing the possible reprisals from Jehovah against this man who murdered God's friend and faithful servant of so many years. The priests confer together before sharing the promises from the Law about what would happen to a son of King David who abandoned God and turned both his own and the people's hearts away from the worship of the one true God of their fathers. The divine reprisals range from plagues to foreign invasions and total destruction of the kingdom and city.

The last time an invading army troubled these lands was near the final years of King Hezekiah's reign. Hezekiah made history that you even studied once in Sunday school in this dark period in Judah's past. He took a threatening letter from the evil Assyrian King Sennacharib into the Temple and spread it famously before the Lord as he poured out his heart before his Lord God and faithful friend.

God had dispatched an angel of the Lord to slay nearly the entire Assyrian host that night in response. Would the Assyrians dare to return after an incident like that scarred their reputation and history? Only time will tell.

6 THE SURPRISE DAWN RAID ON JERUSALEM AND THE KINGDOM OF JUDAH

As it turns out, you did not have to wait long to see what God's response to the murder of His Prophet Isaiah would be. His reaction was both swift and terrible in retribution for the cruel and cold-blooded murder of His favorite Prophet Isaiah. Thinking back on the terrible events the next morning, you are disturbed from your contemplation by shouts of confusion from one of the priests who has just run into the safe house warning not to go out into the streets this morning. When you ask what has happened, the wide-eyed priest shakes his head, apparently still processing what has occurred himself.

A daring enemy raid apparently has taken Jerusalem completely by surprise. Shortly after the city gates were opened to begin admitting the morning traffic, an unlooked-for small and fast moving mounted army arrived in front of the city and galloped swiftly through the city entrance without any opposition whatsoever! It was like the eyes of the lookout guards had been completely blinded in the glare of the morning sunlight. Or maybe the guards had witnessed the untimely tragic death of Isaiah and simply had enough of the senseless, wanton carnage.

Where are the soliders of the Kingdom of Judah? Why are they not resisting the mounted raiders who are riding unopposed through still mostly empty streets, killing anyone individuals unfortunate enough to be outside and to get in their way? They are laser focused in their iron purpose.

If they were hell-bent on slaughter, death, destruction, and plunder, they would not be riding in a tight, determined formation headed towards the Temple complex and the palace of King David above. Yet to all carefully watching eyes, that is what this mini-army that no one dares to oppose is about. They are galloping madly up the hill like their very lives depend on it.

Flitting from house to house and entrance to entrance, you arrive up the hill just in time to witness the small hoard bursting through the palace gates in confusion as they slay the squadron of guards on the doors. Like an avenging angel of the Lord they ride unchecked through the palace eliminating any feeble and half-hearted opposition. You understand completely after the last few days. Who in their right minds would want to die in defense of this monster of a monarch?

The answer apparently is no one. As you stand just outside the palace complex, you watch in muted fascination as the strike force returns from within the palace carrying a sleepy yet terrified looking King Manasseh on a spare horse between a pair of the guards. They have not even stopped long enough to chain him up yet. You watch in stunned surprise for too long apparently. One of the commanding soldiers spies you lurking in the shadow of the gate and makes an instant command decision.

He waves over a pair of mounted soldiers in your direction. You stand there paralyzed in muted fascination as with snarling faces full of rage they seize you in an iron grip and take you before the leader who is anxiously looking over his shoulder and to his left and right for any signs of gathering resistance. Satisfied he still has moments, he is barking orders to put you and the young King Manasseh both on horses with your hands securely tied to the pommel of the saddles. In shock and terror you realize dimly that they have taken you as part of this dawn raid!

You can not even mount a feeble resistance in the iron grip of the pair of soldiers. As your mind races, you futilely think that you did not even say goodbye to the only people in this ancient world who knew of your existence--- the priests of Jehovah. As they are force marching you from the city, you see one of them from the corner of your eyes. It may not help your cause, but someone who knows your name at least is aware of your fate.

He looks aghast at you on a horse being force-led from the city of Jerusalem next to the evil King Manasseh. No one can figure how you became involved in this chaos. You sit atop a horse every bit as much a prisoner as your fellow Manasseh. He stares duly at you, no recognition of who you are and what you are doing as a fellow prisoner dawning on his exhausted and tight looking features.

It has taken only moments for you to go from a stranger in a strange land to prisoner of the hated, dreaded Assyrian

Empire's armies. You try in vain to think of a means of escape, but how can you possibly get away from being tied to a saddle, and even if you could, you are surrounded on three sides by the mounted warriors of the Assyrians. No one escapes from these hunters except by death, you dully contemplate as you recall your Sunday School lessons and history.

You do not have long to ponder your fate. Once half an hour outside of the walls of Jerusalem, surely about to the borders of the tiny Kingdom of Judah by this point, the small strike force of maybe a hundred mounted warriors halts to rest the horses and reorganize. A strange transformation befalls the hapless King of Judah. He is removed roughly from his horse without any sympathy.

A chariot rides up over the hill and meets the knots of soldiers. A strange harness has been rigged up to the wheeled engine of war, with a chain hanging off the back. In moments of horror, you listen as Manasseh screams wildly while they rig up an iron hook and nose ring contraption to the front of his once ruggedly handsome face, ruined forever now. There is a large ring in the front of it, which they affix to the chain and harness hanging from the back of the war chariot.

They untie Manasseh's hands roughly with a harsh laugh. He will need those to keep himself upright you realize in sympathy for the wicked king. They mean to drag him behind the chariot to wherever the army is returning, like a wild animal captured and being brought back to the home city for sport.

You close your eyes at the horror of what this man is about to go through. Who will weep for the murdering monster though, you realize. The screams of Isaiah are still echoing off the hallowed hills and across Jerusalem city walls the morning after that has seen the righteous God of the universe punish King Manasseh for the innocently shed blood that is still proverbially running red through the city streets of Jerusalem.

It has taken the Assyrian strike force less than half an hour to attach the iron ring rig to the face of the once-King Manasseh and chain him in the traces behind the harness of the chariot. You consider how lucky you are that for the moment, the Assyrians pay you no mind and leave you sitting bound atop your horse. If you keep a low profile, maybe you will actually get to ride to wherever the final destination you are going to is.

Manasseh is clearly not so fortunate. You wince as the Assyrian commander raises a gloved hand and the column once again moves out. Manasseh is still strong and able to jog along behind the chariot that promises to be severely punishing if he should lag or fall behind.

It does not take you long to figure out the purpose of the halter ring through his nose and around his face. When at last he should fall along the way, the chariot will simply drag him by the nose to where they are headed. The Assyrians seem well-practiced at this innovative and cruel form of torture. No doubt he would live through the horrific ordeal, wishing with every bump along the way that he had died before he reached the final destination.

You spend the next week traveling like this. Every passing hour lessons any hope of rescue from behind. Who would take the initiative to come after wicked King Manasseh anyway, you realize in silent resignation. None but a few priests even realize that you have been taken alongside the cruel monarch.

As the hot and increasingly hopeless days drift by, you realize that no rescue will be coming from behind. The only thing that could save Manasseh and you now is a direct intervention by God Himself. After the incidents and murders of the last few days though, you can not imagine how a just and righteous God would show pity to the wicked king. Manasseh lived for and loved his senseless bloodshed. Now he will die in it, every bit as much of a victim as the innocent people he slaughtered in sadistic pleasure.

One morning when you are still in a daze, you awaken to see that the destination is in sight. Manasseh's strength to run behind the chariot has long-since failed. He is simply lying there like some abandoned and forgotten piece of meat as the chariot haplessly and grimly drags him along through every bump.

In front of your party is a great and glorious looking walled city. A river runs underneath the foundation of the mighty city walls, atop which you can see chariots riding around the circuits of in continuous patrolling formation. It must be Babylon the great.

Thinking back on your Sunday School lessons, you are a bit confused. The Assyrians' capital and seat of awesome power was Nineveh, not Babylon. In confusion you consider what it means that they have shortened your journey and brought you to the center of the client-kingdom of the Babylonians. It can not be for mercy, you figure ominously. Maybe the dungeons of the Kings of Assyria in Nineveh are overfull already?

Whatever the reason, you expect and receive no mercy upon your entrance into Babylon. On any other day, you would have likely enjoyed the brief ride through the amazing capital city of wonder. Even though King Nebuchadnezzar has not yet arisen to build the wondrous Hanging Gardens of Babylon, the city is already a marvel to behold.

Fountains play in every ancient square, filled with flowers and living trees grow through the stones of the greatest city of the ancient world. Countless acres of fields are actually tilled within the city walls, meaning that this is the first walled habitation built by man that addresses the persistent problem of how do you feed a population under siege. The answer is by growing the food within the walled city. If ever a city were to be designed that ensured it could live totally self sufficiently for decades even, beset by countless encircling enemies from without, Babylon is surely it.

The Babylonians are only slightly better known for mercy to enemies than the hated and cruel Assyrians, but even the King of Babylon can only shake his head at the tragic treatment of a foreign monarch. The Babylonian King will not even see Manasseh and you his apparent minister or manservant. You are made to wait for an audience with the Babylonian king until you are both bathed and dressed in robes befitting your stations. King Manasseh appears that he will carry the nose ring for the rest of his days, for the thing has fused into the bloody pulp of a mass that is now his nose and the defining feature of his face forever.

King Manasseh attempts to recover the fleeting final shreds of his lost dignity as he prepares to face the hearing and verdict of the King of Babylon in his storied Hall of Judgment. The descendent and heir of King David squares his shoulders to face his fate like a man as best he possibly can given the circumstances he has arrived under in Babylon the beautiful as a new day fitfully dawns.

7 IN THE DUNGEONS OF BABYLON

You are swiftly ushered into a bright hall, Babylon's Hall of Judgment, without fanfare. Seated upon a large golden throne covering the central dais sits the man you assume is the king of Babylon. You study him carefully, for it seems he holds your two collective fates in his hands.

As you approach his throne, It is still unclear as to what you are doing in Babylon when it was the Assyrian overlords who took you prisoner that fateful day a few weeks ago. Why they brought the pair of you to Babylon instead of Nineveh their own capital city so much farther to the North is anyone's guess. As you ponder this perplexing fact, you realize that it does not matter that you will probably never understand why.

All that matters now is finding a way to explain to the Babylonian monarch that you were taken alongside King Manasseh by mistake. You are no minister or servant of his, but merely an innocent bystander who happened to be unlucky enough to be in the wrong place at the wrong time.

This will be difficult to prove, you realize as you look down at your royal robes the Babylonian servant girls have dressed you in. Now you are being ushered before the king himself. He confers with a minister who must be explaining the situation of King Manasseh.

At first it looks as matters might go better than you initially hoped. It seems that this Babylonian King is the same one who knew and respected Manasseh's father King Hezekiah. Once the Babylonian monarch had sent an emissary to Jerusalem to congratulate Hezekiah on his miraculous recovery from his deadly illness, as well as one regarding his unlooked for victory over the massive Assyrian Imperial horde.

Unfortunately for everyone, Manasseh took no pains to continue such a budding friendship after his legendary father died. The Babylonian king appears to have taken insult personally that King Manasseh never entertained or saw his emissaries nor sent any back to Babylon himself. Now he comes to the matter of Manasseh's detainment here in Babylon.

It seems the Babylonians really had nothing whatsoever to do with this unfortunate dawn raid on Jerusalem as you suspected. Yet they have been asked as a personal favor by the Assyrians, who are still their overlords in point of fact, to act as jailors to King Manasseh. This is a request that the Babylonian King can not lightly refuse.

So even though he has fond and affectionate memories of Manasseh's mighty father, there is really not much that he can do to help secure the release of you and the Judean king. Uncomfortable as he is to be acting as jailor to Hezekiah's son, the Babylonian king shrugs his shoulders impotently, weakly offering to provide the pair of you with better food and conditions than standard prisoners in Babylon receive. Yet it will not be house arrest or confinement to quarters, no matter how improved the food and treatment may turn out to be. It is still the dungeon of the Babylonian Kings.

As you are pondering the fading brief glimmer of hope that the Babylonian monarch had briefly waved tantalizingly before you, you realize that you have just been sentenced to life in prison without being given the chance of a defense or a hearing of any kind. Even with better food and prison conditions, this will likely mean decades in a dungeon with your only companion the surly and murderous King of Judah. That should give you a lifetime full of regret to listen to whatever is on Manasseh's mind.

You make it a point to take in all of the last sights and sounds you will likely ever witness as the guards are none too gently hauling you out of the hall of justice and down many flights of stairs leading to the dungeons beneath the palace of the Babylonian Kings. In his mercy, the king has given you a cell with a small window that looks out on the city below. At least you have a riverside view of the Euphrates River flowing lazily through the heart of the city. This provides some fresh air and even a few hours a day of sunlight and moonlight, you quickly come to discover as the days begin to roll swiftly by.

Your expectations of having to listen to long, bitter monologues or diatribes from the once-King Manasseh have not turned out as expected. Manasseh appears to be a changed man at least, or a broken man one. Gone is the haughty and arrogant monster of a man who sawed the Prophet Isaiah in half in torment and sacrificed his own eldest son on the grotesque god Molech's statue furnace. In his place is a quiet man of introspection and reflection, who appears at a total loss as to what he should make of his vastly humbled circumstances.

You warily watch Manasseh day in and day out, fearing for his sanity as he sits near the window with his knees drawn up against his chest, pondering the totality of his newfound domain through a little window in the wall, the better conditions for more favorite and fortunate prisoners. He does not appear to contemplate the viability of or hope for escape. Rescue is clearly out of the question.

Even if the people of the Kingdom of Judah and city of Jerusalem knew where their monarch had been taken when he was unexpectedly seized, who would want to go after him and bring him back if they could? Clearly King Manasseh had made himself the most hated monarch of the tiny kingdom of God in its several hundred year history. Undoubtedly, few are morning his loss. Some are probably celebrating it.

So as one day flows into the next, Manasseh sits there and ponders all of these sad truths surrounding the ruins of his life. He should count it fortunate that the Assyrians did not blind him when they took him prisoner and were instead contended with the ruin of his face. Yet you witness a change for the better over the young king beginning one day maybe a week or a month into your mutual captivity.

Manasseh no longer looks to be wallowing in self-pity or doubt. He has come to some grim decision in his heart of hearts and appears to be working things out. Perhaps he is composing something.

For sure he is using the parchment and ink pot and pens the guards allowed him to write something. You stare incredulously at the king. Could he be writing an autobiography of the life and times of evil King Manasseh?

One day when the young king falls asleep at the end of his work, you decide to risk a sneak peek of what it is that he has been so steadfastly working away at. It is not an epic of his reign as you expected. At first you are confused by what you read.

Is King Manasseh having second thoughts about the way he has lived his life and run the kingdom? It appears that way. He seems to have just finished writing a long prayer of some sort.

It looks to be a prayer of deliverance and forgiveness to the God of his fathers. You carefully pry the scroll loose from the peacefully sleeping king's hands and settle yourself by the failing afternoon light of the window to read what he has written. It stuns you to no end.

The Prayer of Manasseh

Lord Almighty, God of our ancestors,
God of Abraham, Isaac, Jacob,
and their righteous children,
You made heaven and earth
with all their beauty.
You set limits for the sea
by speaking your command.

You closed the bottomless pit,
and sealed it by Your powerful
and glorious name.
All things fear You and tremble
in Your presence,
because no one can endure

the brightness of Your glory.

No one can resist the fury
of Your threat against sinners.

But Your promised mercies
are beyond measure and imagination,
because You are the highest, Lord,
kind, patient, and merciful,
and You feel sorry over human troubles.

You, Lord, according to
Your gentle grace,
promised forgiveness to those
who are sorry for their sins.
In Your great mercy,
You allowed sinners to turn
from their sins and find salvation.
Therefore, Lord,
God of those who do what is right,
You didn't offer
Abraham, Isaac, and Jacob,
who didn't sin against You,
a chance to change their hearts and lives.
But You offer me, the sinner,

the chance to change my heart and life,
because my sins outnumbered
the grains of sand by the sea.
My sins are many, Lord; they are many.
I am not worthy to look up,
to gaze into heaven
because of my many sins.

Now, Lord, I suffer justly.
I deserve the troubles I encounter.

Already I'm caught in a trap.
I'm held down by iron chains
so that I can't lift up my head
because of my sins.
There's no relief for me,
because I made You angry,
doing wrong in front of Your face,
setting up false gods
and committing offenses.

Now I bow down before You
from deep within my heart,
begging for Your kindness.
I have sinned, Lord, I have sinned,
and I know the laws I've broken.
I'm praying, begging You:
Forgive me, Lord, forgive me.

Don't destroy me along with my sins.
Don't keep my bad deeds
in Your memory forever.

Don't sentence me to the earth's depths,
for You, Lord, are the God
of those who turn from their sins.

In me You'll show how kind You are.
Although I'm not worthy,
You'll save me according
to Your great mercy.

I will praise You continuously
all the days of my life,
because all of heaven's forces praise You,
and the glory is Yours
forever and always. Amen.

You fall asleep with Manasseh's beautiful and heartfelt prayer
echoing through your mind. In your dreams, you are free once
more, running joyfully through the hills of Judea and
celebrating your unexpected freedom.

8 BACK TO THE CITY OF JERUSALEM

To your undying surprise, the next morning you are summoned again before the King of Babylon. The summons must be good news, for you and King Manasseh are first bathed and then dressed in new royal robes before you are force marched back into the Hall of Justice. The Babylonian King and his colorful court are all assembled together once again as before. In a surreal way, it almost looks like they have not moved from where they were all standing and sitting the last time you were here months ago.

In one hopeful sign, you do not see the Assyrian soldiers who captured and brought you to Babylon anywhere nor any emissaries from the overlords' court. A Babylonian minister whispers to the king a few moments before you are ushered again up to the great throne.

The King of Babylon tells Manasseh he has decided that he played jailor for the Assyrian Imperial overlords for long enough. Since there are no reasonable grounds for continuing to hold you, he chooses to release you both immediately from confinement. More surprising still, you are being sent back to Jerusalem so that King Manasseh can rule the Kingdom of David his greatest ancestor once more.

Manasseh has tears streaming down his face at the pronouncement, and for once he is at a total loss for suitable words. The Babylonian King seems to accept this. He cheerfully wishes the two of you a safe and pleasant journey back to the Kingdom of Judah. It goes without saying that Babylon will be sending a permanent emissary to Jerusalem to avoid any repeat of these unpleasant events in the future.

Just like that your torment is over. That very afternoon you and King Manasseh find yourselves mounted on richly appointed horses worthy of the station of foreign king. The minister from the court himself comes to send you on your way, providing you with both sufficient food and gold for the journey back home.

At first you try to make conversation with the young king. "How did the Babylonians come to decide to release us?" is the query you continuously pose to Manasseh from various angles. He never directly answers it. He leaves it with God.

In the end, you are forced to content yourself with mostly companionable silence on the uneventful journey back to Jerusalem. Less than a month after reading King Manasseh's prayer-letter of repentance, you look up from your simple campsite one morning and suddenly see the shining walls of Jerusalem in the distance ahead. The last time you looked on those walls, you were sure it would be the very last time you saw them alive.

The biggest surprise is that the kingdom seems to have been expecting your return. It was unclear what state you would find things upon your unlikely reappearance, but it seems that Manasseh's ministers have faithfully run the kingdom and kept order over the months that you were gone. King Manasseh sits back upon the massive golden throne of Kings David and Solomon, surrounded by the lion of Judah statues, with obvious relief and joy on his face. He listens with great interest to the report on the state of affairs in his absence. The king engages with several petitioners and ministers, happily granting every request.

Just as you expect the court to be finished, King Manasseh stands up to make a rehearsed speech. He claims to be a changed man since his Babylonian captivity. Time in the dungeon has worked wonders on his heart.

He will govern according to the law and with great respect for the God of his fathers going forward. Manasseh grimly promises an end to the human sacrifice and idol worship, all of which he pledges to instantly expunge from the Kingdom of Judah. He is immediately restoring the worship of the one true God of Abraham, Isaac, and Jacob.

Anyone who did not read his repentance letter would be stunned to hear it all. You think back and ponder his letter once again. King Manasseh really seems to have taken to heart his repentance to God. It will be interesting to see how he carries out these pledges to cleanse the land.

True to his word, King Manasseh starts on the religious reformation straight away just as he promised. The very next morning, he leads a solemn procession into the Temple Complex. It is completely different from the last time that the two of you were here.

There are no longer any roaring furnace gods going this time, no sacrificial victims being led in struggling against their restraints with wild, desperate, fearful eyes. The people are quiet and attentive as Manasseh gives a speech and even reads portions out of the Law of God. You hear him go several times over the portions about having no other gods before God and no graven image idol worship. Manasseh pledges a new era of faithful worship only to the one true God.

He inaugurates it by sending your old friends the priests of Jehovah into the Temple complex to round up all of the idols, false gods, and astrological poles. They collect these in a pile near the Temple courtyard entrance. The king then has them gather all of the instruments and symbols onto the furnace god of Molech, which he then torches himself personally. The ceremony concludes as the remaining melted portions of the old false gods are gathered up and taken out to be cast outside the city of David.

The day after this, King Manasseh mounts up a large escort and leads all of the Priests of Jehovah out of Jerusalem on a hunt for all of the other remaining idols that he himself had personally overseen built only a few years earlier. In similar fashion and without much ceremony, King Manasseh and the priests of God gather, fire, melt, and case out the idols of the false gods. Their priests are either slaughtered in front of their fallen gods or shown to the borders if they are foreigners.

Inside the space of a mere several weeks, the land has been entirely cleansed from the menace of the false gods. There is no longer a statue to be found in the four corners of the Kingdom of Judah. Manasseh has gone above and beyond the call of duty by riding into the north and repeating this cleansing endeavor outside of his own kingdom.

He took his pagan god cleaning crusade into the old Kingdom of Northern Israel and carried it out here as well. The sun shines beautifully on each day, as you can say that God must surely be pleased with the earnest religious reforms of the king. No one can call into question the sincerity of the repentance of King Manasseh now, whose own father King Hezekiah surely must be looking proudly down on his once-prodigal son with great happiness this day.

King Manasseh personally invites and encourages all of the people to come to Jerusalem to celebrate a new Passover feast as he rides around destroying all of the evidence of false god and idol worship throughout the two realms. He has a proclamation read in every town, city, and village to make sure that many people will understand the Passover is the heart of the worship of the one true God of all mankind. Such worship in spirit and in truth can only be effectively practiced in Jerusalem, the city where God promised that He would put His name forever and dwell among men.

You smile in satisfaction at the transformation in the man that you once said was beyond hope of redemption. King Manasseh is indeed a changed man. He is living proof that no one is beyond saving. As long as you live, you will never forget the events of the last six months here in Israel, Judah, and Babylon.

They have been life changing for you too.

You have no other place to be, so you make plans to attend what promises to be the greatest celebration of the Passover since back to the time of King Solomon. And you were not disappointed either. People gathered from not only the four corners of Judah, but also out of Israel in the north to honor and praise the God of their fathers.

The festival goes on for a full week and longer. The only sacrifices this time are the required animal ones to the Lord God of Israel. There is so much joy among the people present that you are sure God has heard their shouts of praise and their fervent prayers offered up to Him like a sweet sacrifice.

Suddenly on the last day of the celebration, you see something strange streaking across the sky. What is interesting is that no one else present seems to have noticed it. With no time to delay, you head outside the city walls through the gates to see what the earthbound object actually was. Sneaking suspicions are not enough to go on where your forever fate is concerned.

As you pass a high hill overlooking the city of David and look down the next slope that looks uncomfortably strangely familiar, you see what can only be the time traveling Odyssey returned. It has come back for you! You cast a last longing, farewell look over your shoulder at the shining gem of Jerusalem as you say your silent goodbyes and climb down to the Odyssey. You are sure that King Manasseh and his people will be just fine now.

It appears just as it was the last time you unwittingly entered the wonder of technology and innocently sat down at the control panel. Nervously you look to see what time is pre-programmed into the dial. To your great relief, it is your own time exactly.

With eyes closed, you lean back into your command chair and await the body shifting lurch that signals a jump through time and space. In moments your life changing Odyssey is at last all over. King Manasseh is once again only a monument of the past, though you know him far better than that now.

The man who became king at aged 12, who revolted against the shining example of his God-fearing and -serving father, who committed more evil against God and Isaiah and sacrificial victims than all of the prior bad kings of Judah and Israel combined, has come full circle at last. Manasseh and the Kingdom of Judah are safe once again.

You realize now that you have witnessed a man's hard-hearted revolt against the God of his fathers, the punishment that befell him as a direct result, and the dungeon-bound repentance that so moved the heart of God that He prevailed upon the Babylonian king to release him and send him back to atone for all of the evils he had promoted for so many black years in Jerusalem.

Nothing will ever be the same again for you personally. Having watched a man whose salvation appeared impossibly far away from reality, you have seen the God of all mankind forgive His King Manasseh and re-establish him on the throne of his ancestor King David.

You can not imagine a more exciting and meaningful journey than the one that you have been on and just returned from now. As you climb into a well-deserved comfortable bed and prepare to sleep like you have not since before you left the modern world, you realize that you have a powerful lot to think about from the life and times of evil King Manasseh and the good God who saved him in the end. He saved the wicked king in every way a person can be saved, and most especially from himself, from the evil lurking inside of his own heart.

Nothing will ever seem the same for you again either, you realize as you fall into a deep and dreamless slumber. In your mind's eye you can still see the shining walls of Jerusalem, and hear the joyful shouts of praise and the happy, heartfelt songs of worship emanating from the center of the worship of the One True God on earth.

9 THE MERCIFUL GOD OF KING MANASSEH

Over the following days as you recover your lost sleep and catch up on meals, you take some serious time to ponder the meaning of all that you saw and learned over months spent in the ancient Kingdom of Judah. You feel you owe this to the journey you have just returned from, for how many people today can claim to have lived for even this amount of time in the tiny Kingdom of God on earth?

It is still a paradox to you how the son of one of the greatest champions of the faith could have turned so hard against the God of his fathers. Manasseh was more than a paradox, born the son of the mighty prayer warrior King Hezekiah who turned out to live most of his life in a manner that offended God more than all of the original inhabitants of the land of Canaan ever had.

Even King Manasseh's very name means, "Causing to Forget!" This name applied to him in so many ways. He forgot the ways of the good Kings of Judah and most especially the successful walk with God his father enjoyed from when he was a young man. He caused the people of the Kingdom of Judah and the city of Jerusalem to forget the ways of the God of their fathers, leading them down the path of terrible and devastating sin. He chose to forget that the policeman of the universe, God almighty, promised that there would be terrible consequences for turning against and away from Him.

King Manasseh learned very personally the price of abandoning the God of all mankind. Yet his life is a paradox in another critical way that applies to you and all of us today. Although he forgot God and turned completely away from Him, God did not forget or abandon King Manasseh. Quite the opposite was true. God used the rebellion and natural consequences for abandoning the shelter and protection of God to bring Manasseh to his knees and into the dungeon where he could encounter the God of his mighty father personally. In the darkest, most unlikely place and point in his long life, Manasseh found God for himself.

The moral of this true story is so powerful for you today, you realize as you turn the amazing journey and story over in your mind again and again. All your life, you were taught in Sunday School that God in the Old Testament was the God of wrath and judgment, waiting on His people to predictably fail Him and go their own way. The truth is completely different from this bias, you now realize having seen it first hand.

You have seen and understood very personally and directly the way of the loving God of the universe. God was never a deity of wrath and judgment, though He must punish evil and sin in the world as He promised to do in His word. Instead He has always been the God of love and compassion, slow to anger and quick to forgive as the prophet Jonah famously pointed out.

King Manasseh is perhaps the greatest lesson of this powerful truth in the entire Bible. The man who you saw repeatedly stab God in the back with human sacrifices, the perversion of justice, the murder of his own son on the detestable alter of Molech, the man who sawed the great Prophet Isaiah in half after his life of faithful service and sacrifice--- this same Manasseh returned to his kingdom redeemed, forgiven, and most importantly of all a completely changed man, determined to redress the grievances and sins that he had committed so egregiously for so many decades. King Manasseh made good on all these promises, proving himself worthy of the amazing love and forgiveness that he received from not just the impersonal and distant sounding God of his fathers.

He received a New Testament level of mercy and forgiveness from his own personal God. Worthy of and deserving torment of mind and body and death in the hopeless dungeon of despair in Babylon, the young King of Judah instead learned very personally that God is good, all the time, showing us all the mercy and grace that none of us deserve. Many theologians will argue all day long that God first worked His mercy when He sent His only Son Jesus Christ into the world to restore us to Himself. Manasseh's life and times fully 600 plus years earlier than this is a reminder that God specialized in mercy, forgiveness, and restoration of the rebellious and seemingly hopelessly lost (the proverbial "prodigal sons") to Himself long before He sent Jesus to know us personally, feel our pain, and forgive our many sins.

Looking back on this amazing time traveling Odyssey you have just finished, it is easy to see how God was the supreme example of love, forgiveness, and compassion to a man who did not deserve anything better than death and prolonged suffering for all of his many actions. It would be tempting to wax self-righteous at this point and say that "I have never done any of these terrible, evil, dark deeds. I could never murder, create false gods and idols, and lead people into horrible sins like this man. I am a better person than King Manasseh any day of the year."

That may be true on the surface, but you are not really any better than the godless version of King Manasseh if you contemplate your own life objectively. You may not literally cast graven images before the great, good, living, loving God of the universe and of all mankind, but you do set up idols in front of him most days of your life. If you do not believe this, sit down for a few minutes and list out the things that you spend most of your free time pursuing.

Now look over the list and be completely honest with yourself before God. Is anything at all of the Kingdom of God on your list? Or is it populated with activities like spending time with friends, watching sporting events, going to concerts and movies, surfing the Internet, sharing and spending countless hours longing for a more excited, wealthier life that some of your so-called Facebook friends boast about on their timelines? Does church, prayer, and service to God and His Kingdom figure anywhere at all on your list honestly? Remember that anything that you put before God, or even that takes you away from God, is an idol or a false god in our modern day lives.

How about a similar list of what you spend your discretionary money on in your own life? Does any of this glorify or magnify God? Would people looking at your expenditures stand back and objectively say, that person is a follower of God for certain? Or would they say, ah, a typical American or European busily spending their free flow cash selfishly on themselves?

What about the country and culture in which you live? It may not tolerate murder, but it does likely countenance abortion, which is loosely acknowledged to be the murder of the unborn in favor of women's rights to choose what they do with their own body. You would probably never sacrifice one of your own children on a fiery alter like the grotesque monster of the ancient world Molech, but it is likely the case that someone you know personally has murdered their own unborn child on the modern day version of Molech, the horrific god of abortion.

The truth of the matter of your own life today as you ponder the story of King Manasseh is that there is at least a little bit of evil King Manasseh in all of us. You may not have spilled blood all over the streets of your own neighborhood, defied God glaringly to His face, killed a person who tried to show you the way to God, or led other people in your own circle of influence astray and away from the straight and narrow path. You have still set up idols before God in your own heart and everyday life, chosen to go your own way instead of God's way (there is no third "other" way), and pursued your own stubborn and selfish agenda in favor of seeking God for His will for your life.

And God does have a perfect plan and will for your life today too. It may not involve selling everything you have, giving all of your worldly goods and possessions to the poor, and setting sail for India or Africa to spread the Gospel of Jesus Christ. It could simply be living your life like a light and beacon to a lost, hurting, and dying world that is increasingly darker by the day as it slowly turns away from the God who loves, created, and saved it.

The great news in the lesson of this story of King Manasseh is not his fall and choice to disobey and defy God to His face. It is that if God would willingly give evil King Manasseh a real second chance, then He will do this for anyone today, no matter how big a mess you may have made of your own life now. No matter how far you have run from the God of your fathers today, He is still standing there "not far from each one of us" (Acts 17:27), with arms open wide, hoping and longing for you to come back home.

Now it is not only God the Father doing this for you, but also His Son Jesus Christ who died on a rough wooden cross for your sins and mistakes that separate you from our sinless and holy God (John 3:16). God the father and God the son are both standing at the gates of heaven which are still thrown open wide for you, no matter how far you have strayed from them in the choices you have made in your own life. The lesson of the life of King Manasseh is that nothing whatsoever, no matter how evil or despicable it may be, can separate you from the love and forgiveness of a merciful, compassionate, and loving God of all mankind.

Another great revelation concerns the deliverance and forgiveness of God. He is full of mercy and quick to forgive (II Samuel 24:14). If you need Him to turn your own life around today, it starts with a prayer very much like the one King Manasseh wrote and prayed over two millennia ago.

The climax of this amazing prayer that has stood the test of time of over 2,600 years (so far) is this: "Although I am unworthy, by Your great mercy, You will save me/forgive me/deliver me!" What did this prayer say that so impressed the heart of God thousands of years ago as it has ever since the day Manasseh first prayed it?

It is both a powerful and sincere prayer of true repentance from the heart. Manasseh acknowledged freely and unashamedly his many sins and begged God to forgive them all. It was a sincere prayer of repentance undoubtedly accompanied by real tears of sorrow and grief from a broken heart.

King Manasseh also promised to change his evil ways before God. He vowed to make amends, live a better life, and serve God. In so doing and saying all of this, he showed "faith greater than a grain of mustard seed" that Jesus talked about over 600 years after the death of King Manasseh (Matthew 17:20).

It did not hurt that Manasseh came from a family legacy of great faith, yet this seems to have somehow blocked and hindered more than it helped him in his own life. Despite this shining example of his mighty Godly father for the 12 years that Manasseh knew his father before Hezekiah's relatively young death at 54, all that Manasseh took away from this great legacy of faith was that it was not for him personally in his own life. If you are looking for the first documented case of the all too common rebellion of "Pastor's kids," you have probably found it in the life and story of King Manasseh, who went as far in the opposite direction away from his father's exemplary choices and life as anyone else I have ever heard of tried.

Whether you come from a long and storied Christian family tradition today or have only learned about the mercy and compassion of our Sovereign God reading this story today, God is equally waiting for you with open arms right now! You have nothing to be ashamed of, nothing you can possibly have done worse than Manasseh that separates you from a loving God who wants nothing more than to make you His child and call you His friend. You can fall down on your knees right now, wherever you are, and go to God in prayer.

The best news of all is that you can have complete confidence as Manasseh did that God your Heavenly Father hears you and forgives you instantly for everything that you have ever done wrong in your entire life!. It is a matter of a simple prayer of faith and trust in God and the saving power of His only Son Jesus Christ. If you want to be reconciled to God right now, say this easy prayer with me right here:

A Prayer to Reconcile You to God

Pray this simple but powerful prayer and God almighty will save you: Father God, I thank you for sending your son Christ Jesus to die on the cross for me and my sins. I believe that He rose again from the dead and is now seated at Your right hand. Father God, from the bottom of my heart I want to repent and ask for forgiveness for all of my sins (things I have done wrong). Please forgive me. I want to trust Jesus alone as my Lord and Savior. Please come into my heart and dwell in me. I believe salvation cannot be bought or earned. I want to accept this free gift of salvation. Fill me with your Holy Spirit. Thank you for forgiveness and Your gift of everlasting life that I have in Christ Jesus.

That was it! Now you can grow in your new faith in Christ Jesus by reading your Bible every day (start with the book of John/Gospel According to John), by praying to your Heavenly Father God as a child speaks to his loving dad, and by regularly attending a Bible preaching church.

And now, May the God of evil King Manasseh bless and keep you and make His everlasting face of love and compassion to shine upon you, and give you His peace both now and always!

ABOUT THE AUTHOR

W.D. Crowder is a six-time American published Christian author, daily devotional writer, financial journalist, prolific article writer, and international speaker. He has penned over 3,700 commissioned articles and written/designed hundreds of financial web pages and newsletter posts.

Crowder researched and wrote his latest book in the island nation of Malta in the Mediterranean Sea, where he lives with his wife and two children. W.D. Crowder has spoken at a variety of church services and Christian group meetings in the United States and Europe and done interviews for a number of radio station programs in the United States and Great Britain.

A widely read and top of his class graduate of Stetson University, he obtained his bachelor of arts degree in History with minors in Latin American Studies and International Relations and a special emphasis in Economics. He was President of his Phi Alpha Theta (National History Honors Fraternity) Stetson University chapter and a Phi Beta Kappa member.

W. D. Crowder has published six prior books in his exciting "Divine Encounters of the Bible" Series, including 40 Days with God (Divine Encounters of the Bible Daily Devotionals), 7 Most Powerful Prayers from the Kingdom of Judah: Fearlessness, Hope, and Miracles for Your Everyday Circumstances, We Three Kings: Two Journeys of the Magi, The Three Miraculous Prayers of King Hezekiah: A Good Man's Example for Our Own Troubled Times, Lives of the Great Apostles: The Real Life Rest of the Story of the Men Who Walked Beside Jesus, and God Will Never Abandon You! Biblical and Personal Examples of God's Everlasting Faithfulness.

You can follow W. D. Crowder's daily devotionals at no cost by going to fb.me/WDCrowder. Find all of W.D. Crowder's books at: https://www.amazon.com/author/wdcrowder.

Reigns of The Kings of Judah (8 "Good" Kings)

Rehoboam (933-916) seventeen years
Abijam (915-913) three years
Asa (Good) (912-872) forty-one years
Jehoshaphat (Good) (874-850) twenty-five years
Jehoram (850-843) eight years
Ahaziah (843) one year
Athaliah (843-837) six years
Joash (Good) (843-803) forty years
Amaziah (Good) (803-775) 29 years
Azariah (Uzziah) (Good) (787-735) fifty-two years
Jotham (Good) (749-734) sixteen years
Ahaz (741-726) sixteen years
Hezekiah (Good) (726-697) 29 years

Manasseh (697-642) fifty-five years

Amon (641-640) two years
Josiah (Good) (639-608) thirty-one years
Jehoahaz (608) three months
Jehoiachim (608-597) eleven years
Jehoiachin (597) three months
Zedekiah (597-586) eleven years

Kings Manasseh's Family Tree

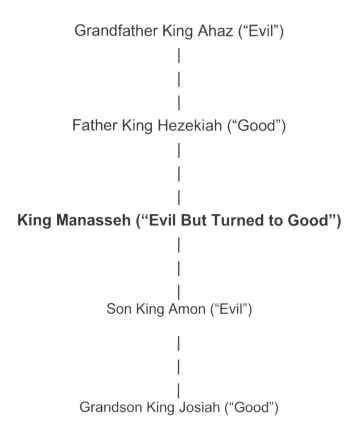

Grandfather King Ahaz ("Evil")

|

|

|

Father King Hezekiah ("Good")

|

|

|

King Manasseh ("Evil But Turned to Good")

|

|

|

Son King Amon ("Evil")

|

|

|

Grandson King Josiah ("Good")

Kingdom of Judah and Jerusalem Maps

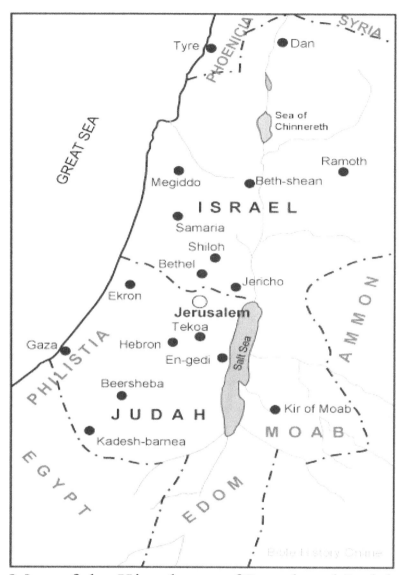

Map of the Kingdoms of Israel and Judah

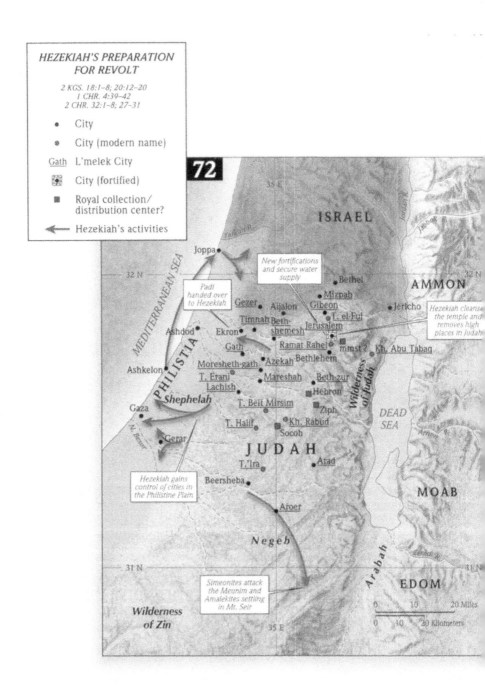

HEZEKIAH'S PREPARATION FOR REVOLT

2 KGS. 18:1–8; 20:12–20
1 CHR. 4:39–42
2 CHR. 32:1–8; 27–31

● City

● City (modern name)

Gath L'melek City

▦ City (fortified)

■ Royal collection/ distribution center?

← Hezekiah's activities

72

35 E

ISRAEL

32 N   32 N

AMMON

Joppa

New fortifications and secure water supply

Bethel

Mizpah

Padi handed over to Hezekiah

Gezer   Aijalon   Gibeon

Jericho

Timnah Beth-shemesh   T. el-Ful

Hezekiah cleanses the temple and removes high places in Judah

MEDITERRANEAN SEA

Ashdod   Ekron

Jerusalem

Gath   Ramat Rahel   mmst 2   Kh. Abu Tabaq

Ashkelon   Moresheth-gath   Azekah Bethlehem

PHILISTIA

T. Erani   Mareshah   Beth-zur

Lachish   Hebron

Shephelah   T. Beit Mirsim

Wilderness of Judah

DEAD SEA

Gaza   Ziph

Kh. Rabud

T. Halif   Socoh

Gerar

JUDAH

T.'Ira   Arad

Hezekiah gains control of cities in the Philistine Plain

Beersheba

MOAB

Aroer

Negeb

Arabah

31 N   31 N

EDOM

Simeonites attack the Meunim and Amalekites settling in Mt. Seir

0   10   20 Miles

0   10   20 Kilometers

Wilderness of Zin

35 E

70

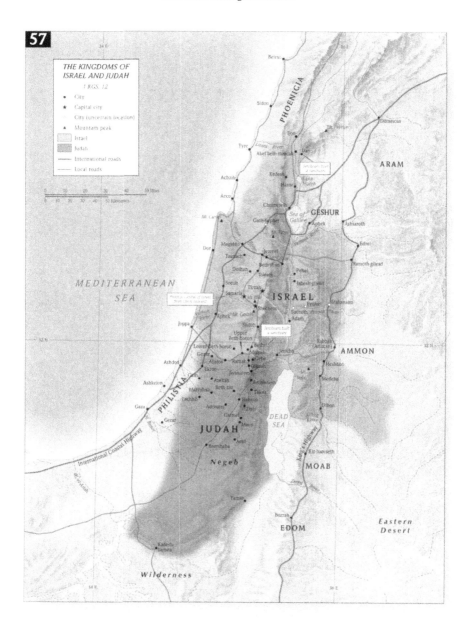

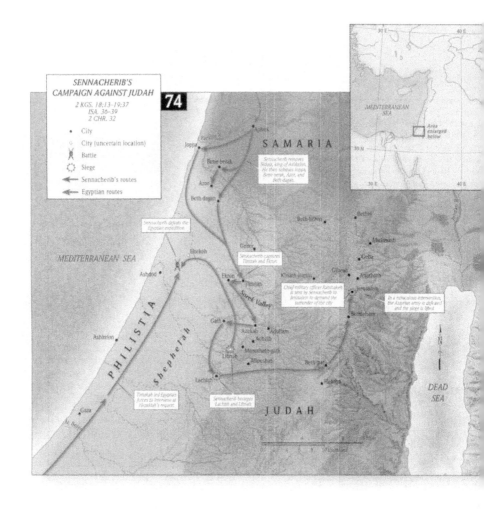

THE FALL OF SAMARIA AND
DEPORTATION OF ISRAELITES

2 KGS. 17:1-6, 24-34
1 CHR. 5:26
HOS. 7:11, 12:1

- City
- City (uncertain location)
- Capital city
- Siege
- Deported Israelites
- Foreigners imported to Samaria
- Syrian captives brought to Samaria
- Shalmaneser V and Sargon II campaign
- Hoshea's messenger
- Resettled Israelites
- People imported from Babylon
- Syrian captives

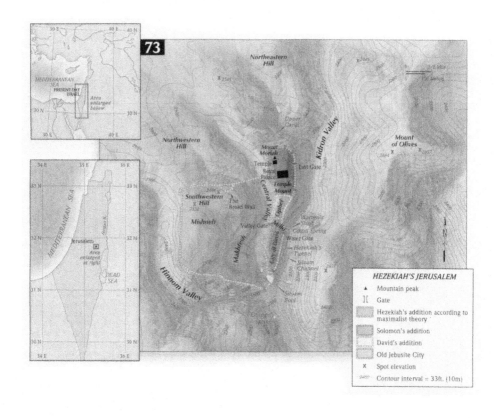

Map of the Conquests of the Assyrians

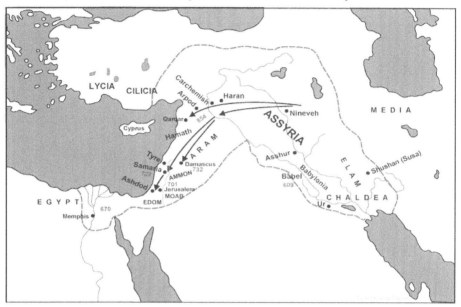

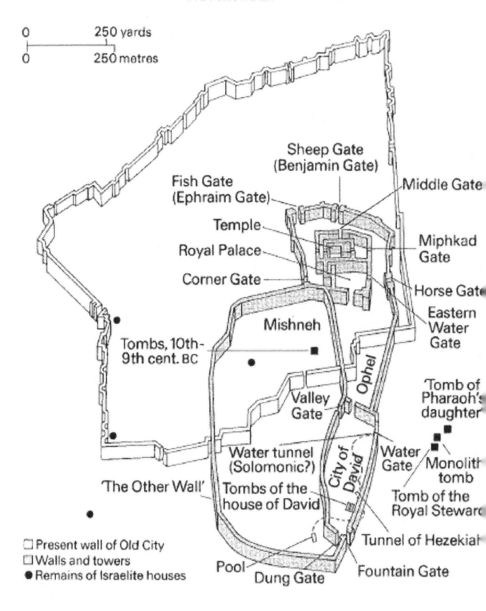

Map of Jerusalem at the Time of King Manasseh

Made in the USA
Coppell, TX
18 August 2023

20523827R00052